T0153997

ADAPT
OR **WAIT TABLES**

ADAPT

OR **WAIT TABLES**

A FREELANCER'S GUIDE

CAROL WOLPER

RARE BIRD BOOKS

This is a Genuine Rare Bird Book

Rare Bird Books
453 S Spring Street, Suite 302
Los Angeles, CA 90013

For more information, address:
Rare Bird Books | Rare Bird Books Subsidiary Rights Department,
453 South Spring Street, Suite 302
Los Angeles, CA 90013

Set in Goudy Old Style
Printed in the United States

10 9 8 7 6 5 4 3 2 1

Publisher's Cataloging-in-Publication data
Wolper, Carol.

Adapt or wait tables : a freelancer's guide / Carol Wolper.
p. cm.
ISBN 9780988745681

1. Self-employed. 2. Motion picture authorship. 3. Screenwriters. 4.
Creative ability in business. 5. Success in business. 6. Social change—
Economic aspects. I. Title.

HD8036 .W65 2013
658/.041—dc23

Inability to adapt is the new illiteracy

ALSO BY CAROL WOLPER

Anne of Hollywood

The Cigarette Girl

Secret Celebrity

Mr. Famous

CONTENTS

INTRODUCTION

I WROTE ADAPT OR WAIT Tables for freelancers, particularly writers in Hollywood who were struggling to adjust to a new playing field. By 2013, the year it was first published, the era of easily gotten development deals was over. At one time you could make a decent living on those deals, and you didn't have to be Aaron Sorkin to get one.

Having navigated the freelance world as a Hollywood screenwriter and novelist, I had stories and suggestions about adapting to the new challenges. Six years later as 2019 gets underway there is a bigger challenge (some would say threat) out there, and it impacts everyone, everywhere. It impacts your job and your self worth. It impacts how you think, how you feel and how you act. I'm talking about manipulation.

Though not always a bad thing and not always a scary thing—it doesn't shake Angelenos the way the word "earthquake" does—manipulation can be as thuggish a bully as you'll ever find. However, in Hollywood, it comes with its own distinctive, seductive, pretty packaging.

Of course as with all bullies, manipulation loses its power when you refuse to give into its charm and / or force. With that in mind, consider this new addition to the 2013 "Adapt " my refusal. Also consider it a brief analysis into the good, the bad and the ugly sides of manipulation. First the good.

MANIPULATION: PART ONE LOVE ME, MANIPULATE ME?

To understand how dangerous manipulation can be you have to start by understanding how much fun it can be. If, in its most benign form, it wasn't pleasurable it wouldn't have the power to morph into something so powerfully negative.

Let me start with a playful example.

For many years, Orso, a restaurant in West Hollywood, was the preferred site for girls night dinners for my group of friends. The place was an oddity in the LA area because it had an outdoor patio that felt like something you might find in the Italian countryside... that is if you managed to ignore the ambulance sirens that came with being situated across the street from Cedars Sinai Hospital. The food was simple, the lighting flattering and the two-story-high tree in the middle of the "garden" made you feel emotionally sheltered from the busy thoroughfare on the other side of the six-foot -high stucco walls.

At many of those dinners, a good portion of the conversation would be devoted to the topic of men. There always seemed to be one girl going through a drama. Might be her relationship was falling apart or she was obsessing over a new guy or seeking advice about how to move from one to the other. Regardless of what triggered the conversation the topic often ended up being about the eternal enigma of relationships and the search for something approximating a compromised version of perfection.

At one of these dinners, we spotted a famous actor dining with his family at a table on the other side of the patio. This guy was a major movie star. The real deal. Not one of those so-called famous people who constantly show up on red carpets, part of a blur of unfamiliar faces. This guy's fame came the hard way. He earned it through decades of spectacular work and an alluring public persona. Before settling down to a life of domestic bliss, he was considered one of Hollywood's bad boys... bad in the sense of incorrigible. He went after every beautiful woman he met, though he never went after any of them for long. Yet, he would have each of those beauties believe she was so very special. Unfortunately, these girls often made the mistake of thinking "special" meant longevity. Big mistake. Ultimately the actor would ease out of the mini affair by saying he was busy with work or had a family crisis or an old friend was in town. There was always a good reason/excuse why he wouldn't be available in the immediate future, which was really just a nice, easy way to say ever again.

And just when the girl would start thinking fuck him, who the fuck does he think he is, she'd run into him somewhere, and he would smile at her like she was the most important person, if not in the world, at least in that room at that moment. All would be forgiven. These women weren't stupid. By this point in their non-relationship, they knew the deal. They knew his words were lines and "special" rolled off his tongue often and too easily. Still, despite this, no one had anything negative to say about him. I don't mean at that table, that particular group of women.... I mean anywhere. <u>Ever.</u> In all the years I've lived and worked in Hollywood, I have never heard one woman trash him and the question is... why?

The answer to that arrived at our table after a little wine and lots of girl-talk. This "bad boy" was able to pull off his fast and loose behavior (behavior that other men in town were castigated for at other girls night dinners) because his charm was so enjoyable. Manipulation that succeeds on this level has to be charming and skillful. This is true in romance, politics, advertising, business, fashion and everything else that involves two or more people with hope and an agenda.

That night as Mr. Movie-star walked through that restaurant patio on his way to the exit, he stopped at our table. Two of the girls there knew him, had flings with him in his predomestic bliss era. I watched as this guy managed to juggle two separate conversations at the same time, giving each girl what she needed. When he walked away both exes were smiling. They knew, at this point, it was just a game but it was a game they enjoyed, a game they benefited from, even if it was just a dose of fun and a momentary elevation in their self-esteem.

It got me thinking. What is the ratio of charm to manipulation? When is charm an undeniable plus? When does it cross a line and become an effective way to confuse and suppress others for the manipulator's benefit? And if that occurs, how blameless is the one being charmed? These musings brought me to this more important question. How many relationships (personal and business) would ever achieve lift-off without a little manipulation?

Artful manipulation does have a place in relationships that range from friendships to business associates to soul-mates. For the purposes of this argument, I'll focus on the romantic, which is an area where escape velocity is an important factor.

To clarify, escape velocity is the energy and optimism needed to create enough velocity to defy stone-cold reality and launch a new connection. Even love at first sight needs lift-off energy. The beginning of a relationship is when two people are involved in a dance that could be called best version of me seeking best version of you. And putting one's best version out there means putting less than your best out of sight. Isn't that a form of manipulation?

Generally speaking, men seek out women who are attractive but not out of their league. Women have to make an effort to look good if they want male attention and access to a desirable league. The effort required (whether it's make-up, botox, hair extensions etc.) can be considered a form of manipulation. Or if the beauty card isn't your game, maybe you try to dazzle with intelligence or social pedigree. Check out Match.com or any other dating site. Look at the photos and profiles posted. People show their best angle. Is anyone saying, "Take me as I am?" No.

Another kind of manipulation helpful to successful relationship liftoff involves what you share and don't share about your back-story. Selective editing is not a bad thing. The person you just started seeing does not need to know the specifics of your childhood or every person who ever ended up in your bed. Getting to know someone requires presenting yourself in an appealing context. (Celebrities walk in the room with appealing context.) Too much truth and too little room for fantasy equals mission aborted. I'm not advocating deception. I'm not straying into "The Talented Mr. Ripley" territory. I'm simply saying harmless manipulation can be a plus for both parties.

This is especially true if you start dating someone outside your usual range. (Age, race, height, weight, personality, cultural background, lifestyle etc.) Harmless manipulation can take the fear out of exploring new territory, which allows you to keep moving forward. You might discover you really are suited for each other and even if you're not, you've expanded your range.

The take away here comes down to this. In every area of your life, you have to be able to identify the difference between harmless (possibly even helpful) manipulation and harmful manipulation. When it comes to affairs of the heart, half the time you're flying blind. Emotions block reality.

The best insurance policy against being on the loss side of the manipulation equation is the six-month review. It usually takes six months into a relationship before you have enough information to evaluate the other person and your own intent, The escape velocity got the relationship going and it has now reached cruising altitude. Time to put all fantasy, wishful thinking and voluntary blindness aside. Time to bring a cold, fact-based analytic eye of a scientist to your situation. Do you like where it's headed? Is it what you expected? Are you brave enough to call it what it is rather than what you want it to be? Is your intent in the relationship authentic? What about the intent of the other person? If the intent is to manipulate for a material or selfish agenda, the manipulation will eventually backfire. I've never met a sperm-trapper who didn't lose more than she gained in the process of getting that baby and eighteen years of child support. I've never met a gigolo who escaped a case of serious self-loathing.

If you don't do a six-month review on the relationship or ongoing fling, you are setting yourself up for being a victim of manipulation, the other person's or your own. Unfortunately, it's far too easy to manipulate yourself into thinking something has potential when all signs point to the fact that you are headed for the deep slide down to some harsh reality. If you understand manipulation and use it in the right way, love (and desire) can flourish. Get it wrong and you're setting yourself up for a life spent veering between fantasy and disappointment.

You might be wondering what this has to do with freelancing and the job market. The six-month rule is one that applies to all areas of your life and is especially crucial when manipulation becomes more dangerous to your mental and financial health.

MANIPULATION: PART TWO SOVEREIGNTY OR A NEW PAIR OF MANOLOS?

The pop culture and peer pressure are two formidable influences. Nothing wrong with being influenced unless influence turns into manipulation and that manipulation becomes toxic. It's a given that we are assaulted by messages all day long... from news and social media, from commercials, from the lectures threaded through TV drama plots and films. Seems everyone has a stake in getting you to think the way they think and buy what they want you to buy

We are also damaged by what we don't see. Selective viewing options are a form of manipulation. Twenty years ago one of the most iconic billboards along Sunset Boulevard was The Marlboro Man, an image of cowboy machismo. It loomed over a key part of "the Strip' next to the famed Chateau Marmont hotel. It wasn't intimidating, it was reassuring. Back in those days TV commercials often featured strong alpha men. Good luck finding one of them now when TV commercials prefer to show us men who are goofy, inept, soft, compliant and apologetic.

You could shrug it off and say...*So what! I pay attention to what interests me and ignore the rest*. Really? Are you that good are shutting out all those voices coming from the pop culture and your peers? Are you okay with NOT going along to get along?

An argument could be made that resisting current trends is not a good career move, especially in Hollywood where in some cases merit might be overlooked because it's more fun to work with people who think like you do. That's understandable. You're in a writing room, working on a ten to twenty episode television series. You're spending a huge amount of time together in the same space. Of course it's more pleasant to be around like-minded people. I get it, but going along to get along creates a conundrum for an artist. Someone of artistic temperament is often going to think outside the mainstream, looking to change and challenge. I'm not suggesting the starving artist route is a more noble and a smarter choice. I'm only acknowledging that since making a living is usually about feeding the beast, it is important to monitor what you're doing so the beast doesn't feed on you.

An easy way to illustrate this is by looking at the world of fashion.

When it comes to manipulation, the fashion world has it easy. All it has to do to get you to spend money is to tap into your inner doubt about how you look. Very few people (and that includes super-models) are doubt -free. So other than those who have checked out of the appearance game all together, the rest of us, from time to time, feel insecure about how we look.

Knowing and wearing what's fashionable is a confidence booster. If the fashion bible and fashion trendsetters tell us pink is the new black then wearing pink is telling the world we are in sync with the trend. Even if you can't afford the three thousand dollar pink coat the fashion editors are telling you is this season's "must have" you can buy a pink scarf at Target.

I'm grateful there are fashion guides to save me from a fashion faux pas. Please manipulate me all you want if it saves me from double-slutting (too much cleavage in a tight dress) an outfit or wearing styles that aren't close to age-appropriate. At what age does one retire over the knee stiletto boots? Torn jeans?

My problem with fashion manipulation is when their rating system of what's stylish and what isn't becomes a force of intimidation—some would say borderline bullying. Enticing you to buy a product is one thing, making you feel bad if you don't is the evil side of manipulation.

I find this bullying especially irksome when you take into consideration that much of what we find in fashion magazines and the Instagram pages of fashion purveyors is fake. An appreciation and celebration of style is very different from presenting curated fantasy as if it's a realistic standard. Manipulation in fashion takes a turn for the ugly when the purveyors create a world that is impossible to attain and maintain unless you're in the top one percent and even then. Nothing is wrinkle-free and flaw-free. Life is messy even for those who compulsively seek to attain stylish perfection and have the means to chase it. In more extreme cases the whole premise of a photo essay in a magazine or on Instagram is a lie.

I once was hired to write a lifestyle piece on an LA socialite embarking on her new life after divorce. When I got to her house—early—on the day of the photo shoot and interview, the place was nothing special. Enter the magazine's lifestyle editor and her team, carrying beautiful decorative pillows, expensive cashmere blankets, gorgeous vases and bouquets of fresh flowers. They dressed the set. What appeared in the magazine was a six-page profile and photo spread of the socialite's elegant lifestyle. I must admit she appeared to be the picture of elegance and entitlement. She wore a Dolce and Gabbana suit and posed in front of an expensive painting that was due to be removed from the wall the next day, having lost it in her divorce settlement.

The message implicit in those glossy magazine and Instagram photo stories is that if you don't look like this, if you don't live like this or, at the very least, don't bow down to the awesomeness of this esthetic ...you don't make the cut. When fashion goes from fun to a snobby elitist dictatorship, who does it serve other than the snobs and those companies making money off of people willing to pay top dollar to enter the snob club?

What's even more delusional about fashion world snobbery is the "Emperor's New Clothes" aspect to it all. I do respect those who have risen to the top of the fashion industry. I respect their skills, their savvy. I have great admiration for the true artists in the fashion world. Coco Chanel was a trailblazer. Azzedine Alaia dresses can make me swoon. What I don't get is why certain fashion editors think their standard outfit of kitten heels and designer print dresses makes them superior to a woman whose daily "uniform" is GAP jeans and a Banana Republic sweater.

Fashion can be a wonderful thing, a way of expressing your individuality and creativity. Saying "that" (to a pair of sexy St. Laurent heels) and saying "not that" (to a lovely but sensible pair of Tory Burch flats) is a way of showing the world your personality. However, love of individual expression doesn't drive sales the way fear and a need to fit in drives the market. The fashion world would be far less lucrative if they were less successful at fear manipulation.

Which brings us closer to the darker side of fashion manipulation. The key question being...What are you willing to give up to be a member of that club? I've met fashion addicts who have no trouble spending money they need for their rent on a pair of Manolo Blahnik shoes. One woman in particular (a freelance writer) was such a slave to the fashion world's approval that she often borrowed money from friends and ran up considerable debt to keep her feet in Manolo pumps. As her debts rose, she reassured herself that any day now one of the assignments she was hoping to get would come through. At a certain point her denial of her actual circumstances became like a bell jar that kept her feeling safe but trapped.

It's one thing to live out on a financial limb and live for the next pair of Manolos when you're twenty-five or thirty. But what happens when you're fifty, still shopping, still terrified of losing membership in the fashion club, still waiting for the next assignment, still late on the rent and still avoiding bill collectors?

I understand that hearing a fashion editor say, "I like your dress" is a high that can make a fashion addict soar. But I have to ask...If push came to shove would a fashionista go with the side that kept her in pretty dresses? Has her moral compass been corrupted by the allure of having the "must haves" of the season? What would any of us give up to get or hold on to our place in the pop culture.

Would you give up your sovereignty?

As applied to writers the question might be...What would you give up to get a TV show-runner or movie producer to like you? To keep hiring you? How many times can you stifle your voice in both work and your Hollywood social life? Dare you say whom you actually voted for? What you actually think about electric cars? Your quirky love for tailgate parties? Do you pretend to be a vegetarian when ordering staff lunches then stop off at In and Out drive-thru for a burger on the way home? If working on a TV drama about cops do you point out that no one needs to see one more chase scene where a cop runs down an alley and catches up with the felon in flight from a fellow officer? Do you dare to say the most popular sit-com on TV has never made you laugh? Not even once. Do you think you could ever admit that though you enjoy a display of Hollywood glamour, award shows are becoming unwatchable, filled with self-aggrandizement and narcissism? How long do you stifle your voice to get along before you realize the beast is feeding on you? How long before it occurs to you that embracing the pop culture's ethos and giving into peer pressure might cost more than its worth?

Getting back to the Manolo shopaholic, she would say...*I don't care about any of that. I love walking into Barneys and seeing all those beautiful handbags and shoes. I love the adrenalin rush that comes with walking out with one of those objects of beauty in a Barney's shopping bag slung over my shoulder.* Maybe her case is simply one of a woman whose adrenalin trigger is love for pretty things. Maybe it was always in her DNA. Or maybe it's an acquired habit, arrived at through years of subtle and not so subtle manipulation.

My own approach is to make sure fashion and peer pressure remain an influence and never evolve to toxic manipulation. If the doyennes of fashion, the pop culture opinion makers, and the political pundits have useful information for me, that's great. If they have constructive advice I can use, terrific. But if they turn into bullies I hit back with the phrase that resets the conversation. *Are you kidding me?* Or, said more emphatically if the bullying is relentless. *Are you fucking kidding me?* That sentence is like a sign saying this is a no manipulation zone. Proceed with caution.

And finally, one more question comes to mind. These fashion snobs who like to throw around a lot of attitude, do they ever consider that, based on a criteria that values cool authenticity, maybe they don't make the cut?

MANIPULATION: PART 3 WORD PLAY

Words are wings or bullets. They can elevate or destroy. In politics and the pop culture words are being subtlety and not so subtlety redefined to serve various agendas. The manipulation starts small with words that appear harmless but these words are not harmless. They are the equivalent of being given piecemeal directions that will eventually lead you over a cliff.

I have done my share of word play. I understand the power of a well -crafted argument to sway hearts and minds. I have used words to manipulate which is why I am acutely aware when words are being used to manipulate me. At the risk of sounding like an alarmist—like a Hollywood writer setting up high stakes in a TV series with a dystopian hook—language has gone nuclear in politics and become practically meaningless in social media.

In the political arena, each side uses words to manipulate voters. Nothing new about that. Usually a war of words in an election cycle gives the Ivy League crowd an advantage. They have the better vocabulary and are usually more skillful at selling their ideas. Except, that wasn't the case in 2016, when word manipulation blazed a new path starting in the GOP primary.

When Trump, not known for his eloquence, scored a bulls-eye by labeling Jeb Bush "low energy," the game changed. From that point on in the campaign, branding "trumped" eloquence. Branding became the sharpest tool in each side's arsenal. The usual crowd-rallying words and slogans were still in the rotation, but they played a secondary role.

Dream. Hope. America. Opportunity. Family. Unity. Equality. Freedom. Liberty. God.

These words could still get a response from an audience but none of these standard rallying cries had the sizzle of a pithy description that branded an opponent in a negative light. Once branding became the lethal weapon of the 2016 election cycle, both sides went at it with full force.

Clown. Corrupt. Misogynist. Crooked. Hitler. Fake news. Liars. Deplorables.

At the same time that branding elevated word play to new levels, it also short-circuited any analysis of the person or situation being branded. Why analyze when you can feel good about a pithy phrase that gives your side an emotional edge. In politics, at least we're forewarned. We know how the game is played. We know an Op-ed is a biased opinion and that news organizations have a horse in every race.

Still, over the last couple of years, when I wasn't being short-circuited by a clever partisan jab, I wondered where this contentious debate would take us. If facts can be branded as lies and lies can feel like truth, where are we? When the definition of any word can be interpreted and redefined depending on an agenda, where are we? If there is no consensus on what a word means, if every word is open to interpretation, then we are on a slippery slope that can lead to making the unacceptable acceptable, and reality irrelevant.

Things get even trickier over on the social media side where we are more inclined to accept someone's personal narrative or claims. This is most obvious in issues that deal in rigid for-or- against terms, using loosely defined words to build walls and lines of demarcation.

In a movement like #MeToo, the words "victim" and "harassment" are often used (and often misused) to suit a specific message and agenda. Are all these women who come forth victims? What about the young (but over eighteen years old) woman who claims victim status because she had a few dates with an older powerful man and after a short fling he moved on? Her claim is that the unequal power dynamic in the relationship renders her a victim. Yet, if she's a victim then don't we need another word for a woman who is raped and held against her will? Does victim now mean any young woman with unfulfilled expectations? Does it mean that a man without power who breaks a heart is less of a victimizer because there is no imbalance in status? Does it mean that men are to be judged by harsher standards the more successful they are? If so, isn't that penalizing success? Shouldn't we at least take a closer look at the possibility that in some cases the man accused is the victim? Protecting women is the goal but can't that be done without a hysterical rush to judgment? Given that Eskimos have thirty words for snow and victims are becoming as ubiquitous as Alaskan snow maybe we need more than one word for victim.

Years ago I occasionally crossed paths with a Hollywood actress who recently (on social media) complained that at the start of her career she was victimized and harassed by misogynistic men. She received more media attention for this confession than any recent work in film. This is a woman who dresses to make the most of her ample curves. That's her prerogative but it is also an indication of her game. In those early years, she was known to practically knock over any competitor who blocked her path to any famous Hollywood "bad boy" who might help her career. Are we right to be at least a little skeptical of her definition of harassment? Of her definition of misogynist?

What about the women who attend marches wearing pink pussy-hats who consider themselves feminists. What does feminist actually mean? A champion of liberal causes? A woman who has sovereignty over her own life? Many of these pink-hat ladies are financially supported by a daddy or husband. Does that mean that a strong, independent, single mom who has supported herself her entire adult life, without the help of any man, is not a feminist if she disagrees politically with the pink pussy hat ladies on some issues?

Victim. Harassment. Feminist. Brave.

So many words have been hijacked by people trying to control a narrative. You could argue that's always been the case, especially in pop culture. However, there used to be more checks and balances on this barrage of information and misinformation. There used to be moments of stillness in everyone's day that allowed for some reflection and processing of what we hear. Stillness is almost impossible in this age of smart phones, myriad TV options and constant news updates on social media. Without stillness, we can get used to words being redefined and misused to the point where there is no longer a common denominator when it comes to definitions. Without definitions rooted in consensus, we are Tower of Babel 2.0.

Unfortunately, the only way to reinstate some kind of checks and balances might be to become vigilant in assessing what we hear and what we say. It's a task. It's exhausting. It's also necessary. " Question <u>everything</u>" may not be a very sexy motto. It doesn't have the tingling effervescence of "find your bliss" or " follow your passion" but it might end up being the only way to ward off toxic manipulation and hold on to your freedom of thought. It's one thing for a word to have a flexible definition to allow for nuance and contemporary influences. It's another thing to be manipulated into thinking the sky is green.

While writing this chapter I recalled this line from a poem by Sir Walter Scott.

"Oh! What a tangled web we weave when first we practice to deceive."

This poem used to be taught to high school students studying the works of Scott and nineteenth century poetry. In the twentieth century, it was the kind of aphorism that might have been needle pointed onto a pillow. Today the web to be concerned about is the world- wide web and tangled information is not only acceptable, it's rewarded. Today if someone gets busted for their lies they offer some generic evasive apology and all is forgiven or soon forgotten. Word play allows people to skip away from accountability and that is a very scary thing.

Going back to that the movie star I mentioned in an earlier chapter, the one who got away with being an incorrigible "player." I have a theory that another key reason the girls still adored him is he never ever abused the word "love." He didn't use it to manipulate anyone. He didn't discredit the word by over-using it. He didn't say it just because it was said to him. By honoring that word, only using it when he meant it and when it had meaning, he maintained a level of integrity and created a zone of clarity.

A few things to keep in mind.

Words matter. When and how you use them matters. People don't like being manipulated. If you try to manipulate them you better be so slick they don't know it or so charming they don't care. If you're neither and they do notice you should hope you never need them for a job down the line. No one likes or forgets being played for a fool.

MANIPULATION: PART FOUR AT THE INTERSECTION OF WILLIAM GOLDMAN AND MARIANNE WILLIAMSON

William Goldman—"Nobody knows anything,"

Marianne Williamson—"God is the electricity, we're the lamps."

I have never been a pessimistic person but I am also not one to ignore what is right in front of me. Living in fantasy always seemed like a waste of time. Not to be confused with creating fantasy, which I do for a living. Given my inclination toward pragmatism the word "God "is not one usually associated with my thinking.

I grew up in a town that teetered on bankruptcy after manufacturing companies left for cheaper options. You didn't have to walk too far down a street to find a church or a bar. I was raised catholic but it didn't mesh with my inquisitive nature. Apparently when a nun tells you... "A sacrament is an outward sign instituted by Christ to give grace", you're not (even as a ten year old) supposed to ask why. Yet here I am having arrived at a point in my freelance career where it has recently struck me that I am at the intersection of spirituality and cynicism.

The cynicism part isn't as depressing as it sounds. My version of cynicism is not so different from William Goldman's oft quoted line from his book "Adventures in the Screen Trade". After stating that "nobody knows anything," he goes on to explain that "Not one person in the entire motion picture field knows for certainty what's going to work. *Every time out it's a guess and if you're lucky an educated one.*

Once you realize that's true, it follows that people are uncomfortable with such insecurity and thus seek out some thing that offers them hope. Enter the **bbd— the bigger better deal**. This is not solely a Hollywood phenomenon but is brazenly practiced here whether it's pursuing the bigger job, the bigger deal, the better romantic partner or an invitation to a better party. Plenty of people believe the closer they get to the bbd the closer they get to becoming a winner. Wrong.

Important to keep in mind that only a tiny minority of people in Hollywood have bbd cachet for life. They reach this status based on their achievements, their indelible place in film history or because they have made the kind of money that affords them a private plane and a boat that could be described as a floating palace. For everyone else the bbd is in flux. People's fortunes rise and fall without much warning. One minute you're running a studio and the next minute you're off the radar. One year invitations to your parties are coveted, the next year you're desperately trying to coerce a B-list actor to show up, promising you'll provide hot girls.

When you are the bigger better deal people want to get close to you. They flatter you and give you things for no reason. You might receive a magnum of expensive champagne from someone you just met and only spoke to for a few minutes. A wealthy socialite might gift you with an expensive piece of art just to be able to drop your name as her friend. It can be an intoxicating ride. Every day is Christmas. The problem is it probably won't last long unless you're in the tiny minority that has cachet for life. A strong case could be made that pursuing bbd status or proximity to a bbd is not a good investment of your time. You end up spending too much time chasing and not enough doing whatever it is you're good at, assuming you have talents that go beyond chasing the bbd.

Often women who marry a bbd realize, after a few years, that they need their own gravitas. They want to be taken seriously. They want a career. Given the trickle down cachet they get from being married to a bbd they can make small inroads toward that goal. Yet no matter how connected you are, how much trickle down you accumulate you can't buy gravitas. You can fake it on your Instagram page but you can't buy it.

Another reason to say no to the bbd chase is because it's not attractive and can be demeaning. Only the most charming or slickest of manipulators can pull off the chase without appearing smarmy. A smart person who dumbs down to get a deal or a date is not attractive. A sycophant, who plays the sidekick role for too long, risks turning into a used car.

Even if you're not a bbd chaser, you can be demeaned by that game. A woman I know, let's call her Samantha, related the following. Years ago when the Vanity Fair Oscar party was held at Morton's, a restaurant in West Hollywood, she would attend with her bbd boyfriend. They were invited to arrive at 5:00 p.m. for the dinner that was served while the show aired on large TV screens placed around the room. This was the A-list time slot. The year after Samantha and her guy broke up she still got invited to the party but they gave her the 10:00 p.m. slot. Worse, there was no VIP parking pass and other parking options were filled. Samantha recounts, in amusing detail, parking three long blocks away and negotiating the distance in four-inch high heels. By the time she got to the restaurant's entrance she felt like someone who took a bus to the event, a glaring contrast to the glittery perfect-looking people who travel by limo.

Once inside, Samantha realized the A-list is mostly interested in hanging with other A-list names, which she no longer was. If you're a bbd chaser getting into the party is worth any kind of aggravation. If you're not (and Samantha isn't) you've put a lot of time and effort into being an extra in someone else's movie.

Twelve years ago, I had the briefest moment of being a bbd for a small number of TV writers, agents and executives. I cowrote a Network TV pilot that was made into an expensive pilot episode. The word on the project was that it was a go. The show's star was a cross between a young Paul Newman and a young Steve McQueen. His charisma was undeniable. The pilot tested strong. The buzz was building. The Network ordered work to begin on the first couple of scripts for Season One. Prior to this positive buzz, I had trouble getting a pitch meeting. With the buzz I was described as brilliant, talented. Producers wanted to "develop" with me. And then defying all positive signs and predictions the show didn't get picked up.

Upon hearing the news, my writing partner (and the guy who brought me in on the project) smiled, shrugged and then suggested we go grab some lunch. Would he have been excited about getting the show picked up? Sure. But, he has a spiritual underpinning to his overview that makes it easy for him to pivot away from disappointment without it registering as a minus. In fact, we had a lot of laughs at lunch.

Being a practical person, I took note of the ease of his transition. Lately, the people I'm most drawn to don't get tripped up by other people's expectations and judgments. And in almost all these cases these people have a connection to some kind of spiritual awareness. They are not the type to sign on to any religious group or movement or to become enamored by some guru / leader / guide. They simply acknowledge a spiritual element in life and tap into it to escape the circular loop of hope and disappointment. Their spiritual awareness helps them bounce back fast and keeps them going strong. Being a practical person that useful skill appeals to me.

This is where Marianne Williamson comes in.

Williamson is a spiritual leader and author well known in Hollywood. In early 2019 she declared her candidacy for President of the United States. I've read a couple of her books but have never been to one of her lectures. I'm respectful of her work but not a devotee. In the area of politics, my practical side would probably clash with her utopian agenda. Yet, she does have some valuable insights and being a practical *and ambitious* person I take note when someone talks about a path to material abundance through immaterial means. I listen because I believe the immaterial is powerful. I've seen its power. Haven't we all (even cynics) experienced a moment that suggests there is a force in the world bigger and more important than whatever the media has decided is the headline?

When Williamson warns about choosing thoughts that deactivate the law of divine compensation, I am reminded that the pop culture is designed to eliminate the divine. It is set up so we are dependent on the media for recognition and approval which means they control the hope / disappointment loop. Ride that loop long enough and you will become too tired to do anything but go along to get along. I'm not saying that people who appreciate a spiritual force in life are smarter, more talented or superior beings. I am saying they are likely to be better at pivoting from life's traps and setbacks. That saves time. That makes you more productive. *That leaves room for magic.*

The takeaway from these fours chapters is that manipulation, in its more lethal form, cuts down on the 'God' electricity. The pivot is the antidote to manipulation. However, the pivot is only something you can do *if you have something to pivot toward that is bigger than what you're pivoting away from.* And what's bigger than God? Nothing.

So it is *because I'm a practical person* and an ambitious one—and because I'm old enough to know what I know and know what I don't know—that I'm making God my bbd. We all need maximum electricity to keep fighting the good fight in our personal and professional lives. With that in mind it makes practical sense to me to make God my bbd rather than any bbd tech billionaire— not that I know any.

You might be wondering how this applies directly to freelance writers. How does this foray into the spiritual zone intersect with William Goldman's somewhat cynical "Adventures in the Screen Trade"? How does it pertain to adapting to an industry in flux, which was the whole point of the 2013 version of "Adapt"?

In two ways.

First, being aware of manipulation makes it less likely you will be damaged or slowed down by it. That leaves you more time and mental space to attain your personal best and find your own unique voice.

Secondly, although Hollywood in 2019 is ruled by analytics, technology, formulas, pop culture trends, political agendas and an obsession with super-heroes, it is ALWAYS in the industry's best interest to be pragmatic. This means it is in the industry's best interest to keep track of what people are looking for to feed their hunger. When Hollywood, eventually, turns their attention to the audience hungry for story-tellers who question everything but leave room for magic, you might, as William Goldman would say, "get lucky."

SILVER LINING AXE

ON THE MORNING AFTER the Oscars of 1993, I showed up at my E! Entertainment Television job and found a note on my desk saying my department head wanted to see me. It was unusually quiet at the office because so many of the staff had worked late covering the Oscar event and after-parties and weren't due in until noon. That made it the perfect time to fire me without causing fear and drama among those who would see their own destiny in my dismissal.

The department head was my polar opposite. She was a paint-by-numbers, upbeat team-player corporate type while I was known for appreciating free thinking, cynicism, and wit. Some might call me a rabble-rouser. Hardly. I didn't have the energy for it. I could barely rouse myself out of bed to get in my cubicle on time. Anyway, my boss calmly told me my job had been discontinued and they were offering me a very *nice* exit package. *Nice* by their standards, maybe, but that wasn't my concern at the moment. I was fascinated by the excuse that they were "discontinuing" my job. I worked as a writer. Were they planning on having all their on-air talent ad-lib? If so, they needed to take a closer look at some of that talent. One girl, in particular, who famously (around the office) thought Al Pacino's name was pronounced "Al Pakino." When pressed on my issue, the department head muttered something about how all writers would now have to edit video that accompanied their pieces. But it was clearly a manufactured technicality.

A little backstory here might be helpful. I was part of the original small group that launched the network in 1987. Back when it was called Movietime. I wrote the very first hour of programming, which was veejayed by Greg Kinnear. A few years after the launch, the Movietime founders sold out to a group of cable companies with HBO taking the lead position in calling the shots. In the early Movietime days the pay and surroundings weren't great, but there was some fun in building a new network—even one started simply as a place to run movie trailers. In those early days, we worked out of a small brick building on the seedy side of Santa Monica Boulevard in Hollywood. The rumor was that it once served as production offices for a company that made pornos, which would explain why porn actor wannabes would occasionally show up at the front door in search of some quick work and fast cash.

Once the big cable companies bought in, they moved us to fancy offices on Wilshire Boulevard. They pumped a lot more money into the operation and then rebranded it as E! It then became a full service source for all entertainment news and was run like a real corporation. Gone was the madcap Movietime atmosphere, replaced with too many meetings and the word "mandatory" popping up far more often than I would have preferred.

My personality and E! were never really a good fit, so I had mixed feelings about being forced out. I was leaving a situation that I should have left years before but stuck with it because I had no faith that I could make a living as a freelancer. I feared that it was *stick with this or wait tables*. Now, I was liberated from those mandatory meetings and had a severance that bought me three months to figure out how I was going to pay my rent. "It was time," one of my freelancer pals said, "to jump out of the airplane and trust the parachute would open." Hmm, heights and trust—neither one could be called my strong suit.

Two decades later, I can now look back on getting fired as an important turning point. I never necessarily had any *deep* negative feelings about E!, or for the department head who got rid of me and who would soon be axed as well. Being told my job was discontinued was essentially a lie, and yet it touched on a much bigger truth. Jobs are being changed, redefined everyday—and so, in effect, discontinued all the time. Corporations have to do what's in their best interest. It's called survival and success. I don't blame them for slicing and dicing. Likewise, employees have to do what's in their best interest, and that means learning how to adapt—adapt fast and always be developing new skills and a Plan B. Everyone has to think like an entrepreneur these days. Getting kicked out of E! was a gift because it forced me to come up with other ways to make money and further my career.

Within three months of being fired I wrote a spec screenplay that caught the eye of producers Don Simpson and Jerry Bruckheimer. They immediately hired me to write a script for them based on an *Esquire* article they'd optioned. A few months later, I signed a deal to do a second script, quickly followed by the assignment to do the production rewrite on the hit movie *Bad Boys*, starring Will Smith and Martin Lawrence. And so it began. Those experiences led to more opportunities, which led to writing novels and television pilots. Then in a moment of full circle synchronicity, in 2012, my latest novel, *Anne of Hollywood*, was optioned by producer John Wells and Warner Brothers—and set up to be developed at E! Entertainment as a one-hour scripted drama series.

Twenty years earlier, I was shown the door. *Now* I was being invited back in to create a show for them. Had I managed to hold onto my low-level writer's job at E! do you think they'd be offering me a shot to create my own one-hour show for them? Abso-fucking-lutely not.

YOU KNOW THAT SAFETY NET YOU THINK YOU WANT...

FREELANCE CAREERS ARE A feast/famine ride. At a low point in my ride, I went to see a shrink even though I couldn't afford it. And not just any shrink. I went to see Robert Lorenz, which, at the time, was like being admitted to the coolest VIP club in town. Picture someone who had the gravitas of a president on Mount Rushmore and the street cred of a Hollywood secret celebrity. The word around town was that a number of A-list Hollywood people saw Robert. In fact, it was rumored that a key player in the movie *Fight Club* was a Robert devotee—a claim supported by the fact that a number of Robert's best known phrases ended up in the movie, including his description of a certain type of woman as "a predator posing as a house-pet."

I had a check for the appointment stuffed in my pocket and was prepared to get my money's worth, knowing it might be awhile before I had the spare cash for a second session. We sat in a small room: Robert in a comfortable cushy arm chair, and me across from him on a leather couch with a skylight directly overhead—not the most flattering lighting in the world, which made me self-conscious. And it had been a while since I could afford the expensive moisturizer and skin products that I so desperately needed. The session was only fifty minutes long and I needed a lot of guidance, so I didn't bother with any of the preliminary stuff about my childhood and whether I was smothered or deprived of parental attention. I got down to the main issue and did my best not to sound whiny.

"Why is it," I asked, "that even with a good education, a talent for writing, a strong work ethic, some decent credits, and years spent paying my dues, I'm back to barely making enough to pay my bills? I'm living in a studio apartment, driving a jeep with no doors (they were stolen and I had a high insurance deductible), and I see no new opportunities on the horizon? The situation is making me sick. I'm an anxious mess all the time."

"What are you anxious about?" Robert asked as if my list wasn't angst-worthy enough.

Acutely aware that the clock was ticking, I skipped over the fact that Hollywood is about youth and if you don't make it by your mid-thirties—or at least look like you still might—doors start to close. Some for good. Some forever. Instead, I went for the more dramatic, Dickensian bottom line.

"I don't have a husband, alimony, a daddy—regular or sugar—a trust fund, or a nest egg. I feel like I'm up there on the high-wire with no safety net."

"Yeah," he said. "You are. So what?"

"So what? So I could fall."

"Yeah, you could," he agreed.

"I could get hurt."

"Yeah, you could."

At this point, I'm thinking, *Maybe I should have gone to one of those shrinks who lies but at least temporarily builds your self-esteem and optimism.* Too late for that now. The money in my pocket was already spent, so I dug in and tried again.

"Well that's disturbing. It would make anyone anxious."

I knew I wasn't telling him anything he hadn't heard before. He'd probably seen plenty of patients/whiners, many of them freelancers just like me, and heard this same lament. The details might change person to person, but the core issue was still the same. I guessed that this repetition is what inspired the polite smirk that crossed his face, as if to say, *Here we go again.*

"Look," he said. "You know that safety net you think you want? That other people have? It's barbed wire."

He said it without great emphasis. No drum roll to a big proclamation. But he didn't need one. I knew what he just said was not only true, but it really got to the heart of my matter.

You're probably thinking that what Lorenz called "barbed wire" sounds pretty good to you. Having a husband, alimony, a daddy—regular or sugar—a trust fund, or a nest egg has its appeal. As do doors on a jeep.

Okay, I give you that. I wouldn't turn any of that down. But I can't dismiss Lorenz's point that there's a downside to having a safety net—or thinking you do. And he isn't the only guy sounding that alarm.

In 2012, David McCullough, Jr.—a teacher at Wellesley High in Connecticut—gave a commencement address that broke with tradition to deliver what could be called his version of the "there is no safety net" speech. Unlike most high school commencement addresses, McCullough didn't stroke the graduating students' egos by praising their grand potential and talent. He didn't reassure them with promises that the right choices and a little luck would deliver them to their grand destiny. Instead, he started off by telling them that, contrary to what their sports trophies and report cards suggested, "You're not special."

His intention wasn't to depress the graduates in his audience to the point where they'd need a Xanax to go along with their diploma. His point was that the assumption that a special life awaits you because you're exceptional and have an exceptional support system could decrease the odds of actually *becoming* exceptional. Overconfidence and a sense of entitlement can lead to weakened survival skills.

Yes, but wait a minute. No matter how correct Lorenz and McCullough might be, their wisdom bumps up against another element key to a career as a freelancer, artist, or entrepreneur. Don't you have to believe you have what it takes to be up on the high-wire in the first place? Don't you have to believe you're exceptional in order to face the "blank page"? Isn't this especially true in a place like Los Angeles, which isn't a city that can get you going the way New York City does? In order to self-start, don't you have to wake up feeling special? Isn't a certain amount of pumping up of the ego required? Isn't a certain amount of ambition-inflation necessary?

Because, I'll tell you, a daily dose of a double espresso isn't going to provide the stimulation needed to go out in the world and make something happen.

So is the mixed message here to be positive but not *too* positive? Whatever happened to "fake it until you make it," which was once considered practically a Hollywood axiom and a popular slogan across the country back in the "greed is good" 1980s? Is it all about being confident without being delusional? I can take a look around Los Angeles and see plenty of examples of those who failed to get that balance right.

THERE'S AN OLD BOYFRIEND of mine—once an aspiring Hollywood player who, at twenty-two, was waiting for his inheritance, both financially and professionally. His dad was a big producer, and he felt it was his birthright to eventually score an Oscar. At thirty-two, he was still waiting and had accomplished nothing in the previous decade except that he got quite good at borrowing money from his family and popping open champagne bottles paid for by other people. The Prince of Potential had turned into the King of Slackers.

Then there's the Hollywood agent whose people skills and charm were so formidable that he was on an early roll in his career, landing a couple of important up-and-coming clients. I'd see him around town holding court at the best restaurants, acting as if he'd soon be able to afford a mansion on Mulholland. Until those clients dumped him for more powerful and prestigious "handlers" and he had trouble adapting to his suddenly silent phone.

Adding this all up, you could say that at a famine point of my freelance career, I had no safety net, possibly suffered from ambition inflation, and had just spent $125 that I couldn't afford to be told what I should have already known.

The takeaway from this is that if some bible for freelancers is ever written, the first chapter should be about the importance of clarity and memory. You have to be clear about the fact that it's a mistake to base all your confidence on whatever safety net you have—or *think* you have. And it's a bigger mistake to keep forgetting that mistake. Your only goal should be to become the best trapeze artist up on that high-wire that you can possibly be. Focus on that and the rewards will come—or they won't. What will definitely come is a greater sense of your own strength and a whole lot less misery.

KA...CHING!

MONEY IS OFTEN THE bête noire for freelancers even when they have a job. Let's say you write an article for a magazine in June. You do the research, the interviews, transcribe the interviews (which takes forever), write it all up and do a second, possibly a third, draft or more. This sometimes means rewriting the entire piece because the editor who signed off on the original angle had a mercurial change of heart. Suddenly the piece about a celebrity's English rose garden becomes a piece about their collection of mid-century modern American furniture. Already the ratio of time spent versus fee to be paid means you're working for lower than minimum wage and the editor never offers to kick in a few more bucks for her incessant second thoughts. Yet, without complaining, you do all the work required and meet your deadline—which the magazine treats as so crucial it's as if the consequences of not doing so will be cataclysmic for the entire planet.

THEN YOU SEND IN an invoice, and you wait. And wait. Days, weeks pass. Finally, you email and you're informed that they don't pay invoices for articles until the issue you wrote for is on the newsstand, which generally means a two-to-three month lag time. That's their policy—no exceptions. So you grumble about it to a couple of friends and let it go. Right after Labor Day, you start checking your mailbox. Weeks pass, no check. You email the business office of the magazine and they get back to you a week later to tell you the check is in the system. They say this as if there's nothing any mere mortal can do to hurry the process along. More waiting ensures and more disappointment.

Often what's going on here is that the magazine has cash flow problems and are waiting for advertising dollars to flow in, but that shouldn't be your problem. You don't go into a restaurant, order a meal, then tell them you'll pay the bill when your cash flow situation improves. The magazine ate the verbal soufflé you prepared, and now they need to pay up. Of course that argument will only guarantee you'll never get hired again.

The typical outcome is that the check eventually shows up, and when it does you become acutely aware of just how little you're being paid for so much work and aggravation. It could lead you to reconsider your career choice or conclude that writing for magazines is a job only rich kids can afford.

THERE ARE ALSO MONEY issues on the higher end of the payment scale. Writing for Hollywood can seem like nirvana in comparison to freelancing for magazines but there are glitches that can create havoc...or worse.

Take the case of a writer, who got a deal to write a television movie, an adaptation based on a nonfiction book. Her agent closed the deal, then gave her the green light to start working on a detailed outline. These kinds of outlines can run up to twenty pages, or more. It can takes weeks, months, to complete—even longer if your producer (or network executive) keeps changing the show's direction. Rewriting is part of the gig. Continually taking apart a twenty-page outline is a life sentence.

In this case, the writer worked for months without receiving any financial compensation. When she called her agent to ask what was holding up her commencement check (due on signing the deal) plus the check for *finally* turning in the revised outline, she was told that the network was waiting for the author of the book—the source material for the script—to close *her* deal.

This is the moment when screaming "WTF" is definitely understandable.

HERE'S THE PROBLEM: THIS particular agent thought it was perfectly acceptable to give a writer the greenlight to work on a project even though deals crucial to the project moving forward and the writer getting paid were still in limbo. An argument could be made that this agent had every right to assume there was no need to worry because studios are usually (eventually) good for what they owe, once everyone has signed on the dotted line. That doesn't mean there aren't instances when deals fall apart and writers are left high and dry with a dwindling bank balance and a stack of unpaid bills.

Example: A different writer, let's call her Vicky, signed a deal to write a screenplay for a film company that agreed to pay her one hundred fifty thousand dollars in three steps. The first fifty thousand was due at the start of the writing process. Hallelujah that check showed up on time. Two months later (and half way through writing the script), the company that hired her filed for bankruptcy, making her deal null and void—which meant the remaining money (one hundred thousand dollars) owed was no longer on the table.

Now, Vicky, being a somewhat seasoned professional, took a "roll with the punches" attitude about it all. Her dreams of seeing her words on the big screen had taken a hit, but she'd gotten fifty thousand dollars for two months of work and it wasn't as if she was in business with a company that was too big to fail. In the entertainment world, smaller companies come and go. She understood the risk when she took the job, accepted the consequences of the bankruptcy, and was now ready to move on, leaving her disappointment behind.

Though as she set about seeking new job opportunities, the producer on the project called, all upbeat and enthusiastic, to say, "Keep writing, finish the script, the project is still alive." Turns out this script was part of a side deal the bankrupt company had made with German financiers. The Germans were still interested in the project and *obligated* to pay what was owed. It's the kind of news that can inspire a girl to go shoe splurging at Barney's. Just to be sure this was all legit, the writer called her lawyer, a partner at a big Beverly Hills law firm, and was told all was in order and that she should finish the job.

Vicky spent the next six months doing two drafts of the script, per the producer's notes. When it came time to turn it in, a big red flag popped up when the producer suggested Vicky be the one to send it over to the offices of the financiers.

This is the moment when a very arch cynical *really* is definitely in order, as in, "*Really?* You want ME to send it?"

Usually producers send in the script because they are the link between artist and buyer, and the last thing they want is to diminish their role in the process. If they suddenly become lah di da about the project, that's not a good omen. Vicky eventually got the producer to send in the script, but that minor accomplishment didn't put a lid on her growing sense of trouble and doom. She clung to the rationalization that her big lawyer at a big prestigious Beverly Hills law firm approved this deal. So she had backup, right?

(Freelancers take note: when you're debating with yourself as to whether you should listen to what you're being told or your paranoia, opt for paranaoia.)

Vicky had her lawyer invoice the financiers for the second payment of fifty thousand due on completion of the script. Weeks passed. Then one day the lawyer forward a letter from the financiers saying they never agreed to pay for this project and have no legal obligation to do so.

This is the point when a request for a double shot of the strongest Russian vodka on the market would not be frowned upon.

VICKY DID HAVE ONE card to play and she clung to this bit of leverage. As a member of the WGA, her union would go after the production company/financiers. That shred of optimism lasted only until the WGA, after looking into the matter, informed her they had no jurisdiction here because the financiers weren't signatory to the Writer's Guild. What this means is that Vicky's big Beverly Hills lawyer, a partner in a big Beverly Hills firm, had no business advising her to work with a non-signatory company. This is beyond a rookie mistake. The very lawyer she was paying to protect her interests had helped the other side gain the advantage through a legal loophole that a first year law student would have caught.

Bottom-line, Vicky was screwed.

» The WGA couldn't go after the financiers.
» The financiers claimed the producer lied to the writer.
» The producer blamed the lawyer.
» The lawyer tried to spin it to make it seem as if the problem wasn't his rookie mistake but the fact that the initial company went bankrupt.
» And suing any or all of them would cost Vicky a fortune.

If, at this point, she started to investigate voodoo revenge rituals to try to score a little justice here, who could blame her?

THERE'S NOT A LOT a writer can do in this situation, but that doesn't mean you have to quietly go away. Remember this: Writers have the gift of gab. They have big mouths.

They like to communicate, and they're good at it. Word of mouth has impact. Tell your story and name names. Tell it with humor for a wider audience. Write a blog. Tweet. Chat on Facebook. Be smart. Don't exaggerate or make stuff up. Stick to the facts. Truth is a defense against slander. If you're part of young Hollywood (or whatever business you're in), tell it to other young aspiring players—writers, actors, and directors. It doesn't matter how powerful the financier, producer, or lawyer may seem to those at the bottom of the ladder. The next wave of stars is coming from those bottom rungs. They'll eventually have the power to pick and choose, and the tables will be turned. The financier, producer, or lawyer will be sucking up to them. But do not turn this incident into a crusade. Complaining has a one-week shelf life. Once the word is out there, trust that it will take root while you move on with your life.

Your efforts won't mean the financier, producer, or lawyer will see an immediate slump in their business, especially if they're attached to a hot property or piece of talent. But when they hit a cold spell (and they will, everyone does) and are stuck with mediocre projects...when a studio or network is debating between moving forward with their project or one by a group of people who have a better, cleaner, cooler reputation...that's when the seeds of the negative buzz you planted can be a factor.

It's very important to keep one thing in mind, though. This tactic will only work for money issues. Trash talking about someone based on how they behave in their personal life will only make you look bad, especially in Hollywood where the definition of acceptable personal behavior is a wavy line. Creative people and those involved in creative businesses tend to be more experimental (some might say indulgent), and that can lead to the occasional episodes of bad judgment. People tend to be more tolerant of those kinds of errors. People might get temporarily upset if you steal their significant other away from them. But if you steal their money, there's a good chance they'll be livid for life.

Remember this, too: Top dogs in Hollywood get to be top dogs by fighting for what is rightfully theirs. Speaking out about money that has been denied you, through lies and subterfuge, will earn you respect.

The take away from this is that Hollywood does have a "scarlet letter" tradition, but it isn't "A" for adultery. It's "C" for chisler. Vicky lost the battle, but there's a good chance the chislers will lose the war.

A GOOD IDEA DOESN'T MATTER...AS MUCH AS YOU'D LIKE IT TO.

LOTS OF PEOPLE HAVE good ideas. Lots of people have ideas that could potentially make a lot of money. These kinds of ideas, when told, often garner responses, such as: *You should do that, make that, sell that. I'd buy that, watch that, join that club.* Most of these ideas go nowhere because an idea is only as valuable as its potential velocity. It isn't rare for someone to come up with an idea that sounds like a top ten television idea or a hit movie. It is rare for that great idea to be worth anything unless backed by the creator's follow-through. Turning an intangible into a concrete product is the most valuable skill for any freelancer, and there are plenty of examples around (especially in the entertainment business) of a mediocre idea with follow-through being far more valuable than a great idea without any.

A most recent example of that is the bestseller *Fifty Shades of Grey* by E. L. James. A huge hit, and yet any one of the women at my girls' lunches or dinners could come up with a more erotic tale based on their own actual experiences. If you pushed them to go into the realm of their imaginations, the stories they could tell would be plenty times more sizzling and provocative. Yet, these women never considered their real or imagined sexcapades were worthy of attention, and coming up with the kind of quasi-erotic romantic fantasy that E. L. James excels at doesn't speak to them. Watching ten seconds of Rihanna dancing in one of her videos is far more erotic to me than reading about the fictitious Anastasia Steele's flirtation with S&M. But *Fifty Shades* has found its audience, doing it through tons of viral marketing, and that's a triumph for follow-through over intellectual ennui.

OVER THE COURSE OF my writing career plenty of non-writers have approached me with this proposition: "I have a great idea for a show we should do together." First of all, most writers have dozens of their own ideas which they plan to work on as soon as they have a free moment. Secondly, working on someone else's idea without getting paid does not make me a happy girl. Nor does it make my bill collectors happy.

Too often, the idea person thinks that simply having the idea is doing their part. They think they've already contributed their 50 percent—some think the idea is 90 percent—and all the writer is doing is filling in the blanks. These people don't understand that having the idea is really just the fun part. If feels good. It's a champagne high. People give you props for your creativity. They tell you how clever you are and laugh at your snappy insights.

Taking that idea and turning it into something that might be sellable does not, for the most part, feel good. Unless you're the rare person who finds slogging through mud until your legs cramp up, looking for a needle in a haystack to the point of eye strain, and working on a challenging Suduko puzzle until it brings on a major migraine is your idea of a fun adventure.

Let's say the idea pitched to you strikes you as unique and potentially commercial. Let's say the concept is this: a four-hundred-dollar-an-hour New York City therapist encourages his patients to lie without guilt as part of their therapy, and he soon becomes the go-to guy for Wall Street billionaires and high-end grifters.

You might say, "Okay, I can see this as a series for cable." And your brain starts firing away. You imagine a guy like Dennis Leary or David Duchovny as the therapist who you picture as a super-smart forty-ish guy, part shrink, part guru. He never acknowledges that he encourages his patients to lie. Instead, he says he's helping them to manage reality. He makes a good case for why standard rules for lying are repressive and what matters is the bigger truth...whatever that bigger truth is. It's easy to imagine a few of his patients getting into trouble following his advice, and yet others are the ones who inevitably thrive. It all comes to a fiery finale when the managed reality clashes with unmanageable reality for what television execs like to call "episodic satisfaction."

Against your better judgment, developing someone else's idea is usually a nightmare: you decide to say yes, the idea person goes away happily leaving you to do the heavy lifting—and, make no mistake about it, it is always heavy.

To fully flesh out the idea, you have to know who all the characters are, how they will interact with each other, and what stories their interaction will inspire.

You have to figure out the theme and tone of the show, the pilot episode, and the overall arc of the first season. You need to have at least a few plotlines worked out that'll carry the show into its second year and beyond—making sure they are intriguing enough to convince the idea-buyers that this concept has what it takes to keep viewers hooked.

Let's say you do all that and now you want to pitch it to a development executive. Let's say you have an agent and run it by them. They say, "Let me think about which networks might be interested." When you don't hear back right away, you email. Eventually, the agent replies with this advice: they tell you the best way to go is to attach a producer who has a track record in television, and then they ask if you have any producer friends who might be interested.

You do your best *not* to say, "Am I missing something here? Aren't *you* supposed to be matching *me* up with producers in your stable of clients?" But you don't vent. Instead, the conversation ends with them telling you they'll give it some thought and get back to you.

Meanwhile, the idea person calls for a progress report. You give them the update, and they seem surprised that you don't have better connections in the biz. You can practically hear them thinking, *Did I take my brilliant idea to the wrong person? Did I waste my brilliant idea on someone who is a loser?*

They don't come out and say that, but they do act as if—by virtue of them checking in with you—they've done their latest share of the follow-through. More like a drive-thru, but you let it go and keep pestering your agent until they eventually set up a pitch meeting with a production company that has a first look deal with Showtime.

On the day of the pitch, it's raining hard and you get stuck in sluggish rush hour traffic. It takes you an hour to commute to their offices in the Valley. You're scheduled to meet with three people, only one who has the power to say yes or no. When you walk into the room, that person is absent. Her underlings apologize and say she's sick or she had a family issue or a work emergency. Doesn't matter what the excuse is because you're not paying attention since it has just dawned on you that this meeting was agreed to as favor to your agent. They have no intention of buying your pitch. They agreed to hear it only to curry favor with your rep in case they need their help on another project down the line. In other words, your agent got you this faux meeting to get you off their back and maybe because they feel sorry for you. Truth is, you don't have enough cachet to attract a big shot producer. You've heard of pity fucks? Think of this as a pity pitch.

You give it your all anyway, and to your shock and delight the underlings say they love it and are going to schedule a time for you to come back and meet with their boss. For twenty-four hours you're hopeful—until your agent calls to say they loved you, you did a great job, but that it's not what they're looking for right now.

Not what they're looking for right now? They had been given a description of the idea before you ever met with them. Were they open to shrink ideas on a Friday, but then only into cop ideas the following Monday? This is when you start to realize—and almost in a perverse way have an appreciation for—the fifty euphemisms for rejection. Not willing to give up, you eventually toss pride out the window and contact an executive you once worked with at another network, convincing him to give you a shot. Another room, another couple of underlings who also say they love it. But this time add that they've just bought something similar from a writer who does have a big shot producer attached to his project. Fifty ways to be rejected. Fifty bumps in the road. This is the point when you could give up, and most people would say you followed through as far as you could, and that there's no shame in giving up. They would be wrong.

Take a step back and look at where you have been, and where else there is to go. You have been rejected by people working within an established system. Even very successful established systems don't get to escape the laws of the universe, which tells us everything is in a state of flux. There was once a time when a deal at a record company was the only way to get your music to a wide audience. Then technology and the internet came along, and those seemingly invincible giant companies had to play catch up. A one-time host of KCRW's critically acclaimed show *Morning Becomes Eclectic* once told me that it reached a point where there was a greater chance the next piece of music that got him excited would be a homemade CD handed to him by a stranger in the bathroom at the Troubadour than a submission from a major established record company. Good ideas have a much longer shelf life these days as long as you know where to go.

> » Fifty ways to be rejected
> » Fifty bumps in the roads
> » *But also...*
> » Fifty exits off rejection highway

In the case of this apocryphal television idea, there are options. You can take that idea and turn it into a novel. Turn it into a non-fiction article about guru shrinks. Write a blog for site that is the equivalent of a pop culture magazine. See how many hits you get. Once you have something in print, something tangible, people are more likely to take you seriously. Based on the responses and comments posted you can shape the idea into a more sellable package. If you can afford to, make a five-minute video of the shrink character and put it on YouTube. If money is an obstacle, find out who the big buyers are in short-form series online and submit it as an idea. Pay attention to what's happening in the world, and see if your bestselling tool is today's headlines. When Eliot Spitzer was caught dallying with a hooker, call girl shows that were going nowhere found new life on cable. Or you can take one character you created for the shrink show and spin it off into another pitch for a younger audience. How about a show about a seventeen-year-old girl whose dad is a guru shrink specializing in rationalizing bad behavior? This "education" gives her the knowledge and license to become a monster of manipulation. Dreiser's Becky Sharp on steroids.

Of course, follow-through is made easier if you hook up with the right partner. Whether it's the person who brings you the idea, or the producer you bring the idea to, there are certain kinds of partners to avoid because they are follow-through blockers.

Watch out for the immediate gratification junkie. One of my favorite stories about this type of personality is a guy, possibly in his mid-twenties, who was blessed with panache and a Hollywood pedigree. People assumed he could get stuff done. Wrong. His problem was that he lacked the discipline to stay with a project once the endorphins eventually wore off. The classic story about him came from his ex-wife who tells the tale of their first Christmas as a married couple. At his parents fancy gift-opening party, he (only in his early twenties at the time, so you have to give him some slack for immaturity) hands her a fancy small box. Inside is a check for a thousand dollars, and a letter, which he insists she read aloud with his parents and siblings present. The letter says that this check is just a tiny first step in the savings account he's set up for their future kids and their life together. Sappy but sweet. He is immediately given love and approval from all present. A month later the ex-wife comes across a bank statement that shows he withdrew the money and closed the account. Turns out, he spent the cash on drugs and new tech toys. For people like this, down the line gratification requires too much patience and work. These people have no interest in a finish line unless it's right there in front of them and they can already hear the crowd's applause. It was a pattern this guy played out personally and professionally over and over again.

The other type of partner to avoid is the coward afraid of being judged. There are a lot of these in the freelance world, and some of them have terrific, original, fresh ideas. But they never want to turn in the project. They will work on it forever. Fine-tuning. Second-guessing. Rewriting. Their terror is that, once they turn it in, they will lose control and could be open to stinging criticism—which is, of course, true. There's no guarantee the response will be positive. You might be dealing with an executive who earned their position solely based on corporate politics. They may not be trained to judge a project based on its artistic merits. Their goal is to choose the project (a variation of something that's already succeeded) most likely to keep them from losing their job. They're less open to innovative work. I understand. No one wants to lose their livelihood. If I'm dealing with this type of executive, I don't expect praise and acceptance if I turn in work outside the traditional grid. I realize the odds are against me, but I'm still willing to play the odds. Unfortunately, the coward can't follow-through without coddlign and encouragement. Guaranteed.

Then there's the type that might be the biggest threat to follow-through: the low self-esteem partner. Though sharing some characteristics with the coward, the low self-esteem type never gets close to the finish line. There is no second-guessing or endless fine-tuning because they quit halfway through the assignment. Fearing they're not good enough, they find ways to sabotage any progress. Often they start off strong, gung-ho, and somewhere in the middle of the work they'll manufacture a drama. If they have kids, that'll inevitably be a great excuse. Their son has a problem at school. The nanny quit. Their daughter is now into volleyball and has to be driven all over Los Angeles County to compete. They promise to get back into the project once the drama has passed, but what they really want is for it to fade away so they can continue to maintain the illusion that they're serious about working and being professional without ever dealing with the real reason they never go the distance.

The takeaway from this is that if you have no follow-through, you better learn how to acquire it, or only partner up with people who have it. Or get out of the freelance game, get a normal job that doesn't require as much of this skill. Or hope that you're very, very lucky and will find yourself in the right place at the right time. Pray that opportunities will drop into your lap and you won't need follow-through. At least not at first. But even if you are blessed with that luck and you find success young—even if at twenty-five you're plucked out of the chorus and made a star—sooner or later you're going to need to learn how to adapt and follow through.

When the going gets tough, freelancers have to get tougher. You have to look those naysayers in the eye, thinking to yourself: *Fuck it. They don't get it. Fine. They're not the only casino in town.*

THE DADDY FACTOR

*I*N MY TWO DECADES as a freelance writer, it has been men more often than women who supported and promoted me. And in a couple of cases, became an unofficial mentor.

Though these men weren't all decades older, their level of success made them a kind of daddy figure. Not to be confused with a sugar daddy. Sugar daddies buy you things in return for sex. That's more like bribery. Mentor daddies require no sex and give you advice so you can succeed and buy your own things. That's more like nurturing.

Now, I know what you're thinking. That, even if mentor daddies aren't swapping guidance for sex, there's still a sexual component, attraction, or fantasy to the hook-up.

There may be some truth to that, but it isn't necessarily true. And as long as it's not a manifested part of the relationship, who cares? In my personal case, I've never dated my mentors. I'm not their type. Not tall enough. Not blonde enough. Not glam enough.

Valuing male mentors as I do doesn't mean I haven't worked with some fabulous women. I have had the good fortune to work with talented female writers, producers, executives, and editors. In a couple of cases, I would even go so far as to refer to them as angels. Yet, looking at things through a wider lens, I can't ignore the obvious facts and avoid drawing the conclusion that dare not be mentioned around any self-proclaimed feminists. The truth is, there is a natural competitiveness women feel with their own gender that can result in working against—not for—their "sisters." Or as my therapist once said, "Girls get along until they are vying for the same size candy bar." And if you add a man into the picture, sisterhood goes out the window. "It's in the DNA," he used to say. Thousands of years of DNA memory still impact how women behave today. Competition for male attention was once tied to survival, and though that's no longer the case on a life or death level, instincts die hard. The plot of the movie *Mean Girls* might be hilarious, but it's no joke. Women carry the chip to be a bitch, and in the competitive business world that's data that shouldn't be ignored.

On the other hand authentic male mentors aren't worried that young woman they've taken under their wing will outshine them. They wouldn't be alpha if they were. These men are wired to understand that helping new talent enhances their own power. They know how to enjoy the thrill that comes with being smart enough to recognize and encourage young talent as much as they enjoy being the savvy guy in the room who bought a low-trading stock before it skyrocketed. Though the *A Star is Born* scenario happens on occasion, those rare occasions tend to be in an entertainment world that craves new scenery and is shaped by pop culture. A case could be made that one of George Clooney's girlfriends could become—if she got a stellar part in a movie, a prestigious modeling gig, etc.—a bigger star than George. But Hillary Clinton, even if she eventually becomes president, will never really outshine Bill.

The mentor relationship doesn't work the same way in girl world because women want the low-trading stock they bought to stay low. Rarely do you find (I've never found one) mentor mommies in a highly competitive world. Women might love and praise you as a great assistant, but chances are they will love you less if you climb the ladder to success.

I saw this early on in my career when I witnessed the bad behavior of a Hollywood "player." Let's call her boss lady Kate. She hired a recent college graduate—let's call her Jane—to help develop projects, bring in scripts, and work with the writers. At first, she saw herself as Jane's mentor. Jane was her mini-me, and she liked being able to count on her for intelligent feedback and her ability to get a script in shooting shape.

Good news for all? Apparently not for Kate. As Jane's talents became known throughout the industry, she had other job offers and decided to pursue a particularly good one. The day Jane left Kate's company, Kate reacted with a string of expletives that made me wonder if she was having some kind of 'roid rage. There are rageaholics in Hollywood, but I got to tell you that seeing a woman go that psycho is not pretty, definitely not necessary, and always works against her in both the short and long term.

Kate practically waged a war against Jane, until her ex-assistant became so successful Kate's attacks looked crazy and vindictive. Only then did she tone down the insults and attempt to rewrite history by reminding everyone she trained Jane. Guess she was thinking that if she couldn't destroy Jane's success, the next best thing would be to try to claim credit for it.

I experienced a similar kind of sisterhood backlash when I published my first novel, *The Cigarette Girl*, in 1999. My editor made up a list of known women authors we hoped would read my book and give me a blurb for the back cover. We targeted writers who had written books in the same genre (back then it was called chick lit) as my novel. Not one woman agreed to give me a quote—though later on my work was embraced by *Vogue*, *The Washington Post*, *Entertainment Weekly*, and plenty of other critics (male and female) both in the US and in Europe. But here's who did offer a blurb: Bret Easton Ellis. I didn't know Bret back then, and there was no reason for him to go out of his way to give me a wonderful endorsement which helped my book get attention, but he did. My fellow chick lit writers were just not about to help a new voice in the marketplace. Maybe if I had had a powerful husband who ran a studio and they thought by sucking up to me one of their books might get optioned, then they would have been inclined to give me a gushy quote. But as an unknown potential competitor in their niche of the market, it wasn't going to happen. Their silence spoke volumes.

There's one more area of sisterhood backlash that I should mention, and beware, this is the most politically incorrect part of the chapter. If an insecure, unattached woman in a position of power sees you as the kind of woman that can attract the attention of the men who rejected her, she will feel less inclined (to put it mildly) to help you no matter how qualified for the job you might be. It's a variation of "the enemy of my enemy is my friend." In this case, it's "the object of lust of my *unrequited* object of lust is my enemy." If a powerful woman sees that the alpha male she wants attention from is focusing attention on you—even though there is no sexual relationship going on—don't expect any promotions.

YOU MIGHT BE WONDERING where one finds one of these alpha mentor daddies.

The problem is you can't go out shopping for one. All you can do is put yourself in an arena where meeting one is more likely to happen. It's probably not going to happen in a small town on the verge of bankruptcy. It can happen in New York City, Los Angeles, Miami, San Francisco, wherever. Go where the money and the power is and keep developing your skill set. And by skill set, I don't just mean your career. Build an interesting life, a circle of interesting friends, and compelling interests. You have to capture someone's attention before you can talk to them about your work. Men are visual creatures. Look good. You don't have to look like Charlize Theron, but a little mascara can go a long way. More importantly, be passionate and committed. Los Angeles is filled with dreamers who talk a good game. I know people who can go on and on about their travels and their busy, busy work itinerary, and all the projects they're working on. It can all sound impressive, at time intimidating, but alpha male daddies are sharp. They know the difference between passionate talkers and passionate doers.

IF YOU ARE FORTUNATE enough to find a male mentor, there are a few things to keep in mind:

» Pay attention to their advice. You don't have to agree with every single thing they say, or act on every one of their suggestions, but if they feel they are talking in vain, they'll move on.

» Be witty, entertaining, and curious. Humor is energy. Clever repartee is energy. Being open and curious and knowledgeable about new things going on in the world is energy. Young people have an excess of energy and they don't yet understand the shortage of that life force that will come with age. In this regard, youth is in the leverage position. Energy is what you can give back in return for the sage guidance you're getting from your older, wiser mentor. You are out there on the streets. They are up there on their mountaintop. You can be their guide to what's happening in your generation. You can be their guide to what the future holds.

» And, above all, remember that an alpha male daddy is not actually your daddy. Don't dump your personal problems on him. He's not there to pay your rent, give you a pep talk when you're having a bad day, or bail you out of jail if you get pulled over for a DUI.

Keep in mind, failure to recognize the boundaries of the mentor relationship can result in being replaced by someone who is twice the fun and half the headache.

KNOWING NO ONE

*R*ECENTLY I READ *New York Magazine*'s spring fashion issue which featured a glowing article about Oscar de la Renta, including accolades from some of his favorite clients and friends. The gorgeous Lauren Santo Domingo, a contributing editor at *Vogue*, recounts how, upon her graduation from college, she wanted the job that (according to her) every girl wants—*Vogue* fashion assistant. She interviewed and never got a call back. Weeks passed. She was devastated. Seeing her devastation, her future mother-in-law, Beatrice Santo Domingo, stepped in and put in a call to her good friend Oscar, who put in a call to *Vogue*, and...*voila!*...Lauren got the job.

Nepotism is a fact of life, and there's nothing wrong with that. I don't resent Lauren for having an advantage, and though fashion is not my area of expertise (jeans, shirt, and boots are my fashion uniform components) I'm sure she's talented and fits right into the *Vogue* culture. My concern is for the person who is equally as talented as privileged girls like Lauren but, unfortunately, knows no one who knows someone who can make that all important call to *Vogue*.

As a freelancer, I know scoring an assignment (or staff job) with a major magazine is no easy feat. Editors like to work with people who are already established, people they know and believe in, and/or people being touted as the next new thing. But how do you become the next new thing when no one will give you a chance to show your thing?

IF YOU HAVE NO connections, it can be painful to watch others get ahead when you know you're just as capable. Even worse is to watch someone who doesn't have the skills and still gets to move to the front of the line.

I once dated a guy who grew up in the upper tier of the Hollywood biz and had an extensive network of contacts. When this boyfriend got out of college, he immediately got a low-level but highly-coveted job on a big budget movie. It was meant to be temporary, the way a titan of industry might have his heir briefly work in a non–executive capacity to get a sense of the business from the bottom up. It was more like a summer apprenticeship than an actual job. From there my boyfriend landed at a television network, which is what he was doing when I met him. He was responsible for developing new projects, a position that was supposed to fast track him to a senior exec role.

Problem is he wasn't good at his job and hated reading scripts. To help him out, I ended up doing the coverage on all the screenplays he brought home. He took my notes and passed them off as his own. His boss loved the coverage, which was ironic because had I applied for that very job I never would have been hired. I didn't have the trickle-down cachet that was my boyfriend's birthright and was obviously an important factor on a job application. My guy had the connections, but no skills. I had the skills, but no connections. We were either a perfect match or a disaster waiting to happen.

Ultimately, I went on to make my own connections, and he went on to find other girls to do his work for him. I don't feel taken advantage of because I honed my script analysis skills doing his "homework," and I learned a lot about how that particular network functions. Adding to your knowledge of the game is never a waste of time. Knowing as much as you can about the lay of the land leads to confidence. When you walk into a meeting and you know what the deal is, then the person on the other side of that desk becomes less intimidating. Regardless of their power and their ability to buy or pass on an idea, they too are a cog in the industry wheel—and keeping that in mind makes for a more relaxed pitch. You're not pitching to God. You're pitching to someone desperately seeking their next hit. In Hollywood (and in business), you're only as good as what you've done lately. And as much as a buyer might be reluctant to say yes to your idea, they are also panicked that they'll say no to something that will turn out to be the next *Homeland*, *Sopranos*, Facebook, or Twitter.

That said, it's not easy being the one who is struggling when you're surrounded by those who are thriving because they had the good fortune to have a connection to "Oscar." I remember once being at lunch with a group of women who were all in good career situations because of who they married. They all enjoyed the perks that came from their exalted positions, and were all dressed in Lanvin or Dolce or Prada. That day the topic of conversation was which Four Seasons hotel had the best accommodations. While they chatted about spa services and cuisine, I sat there distracted, wondering if I had enough in my checking account to pay that month's cable bill.

It took me years before I realized that instead of sitting there feeling like a loser, I should be filled with pride. So many people on the others' ninety yard line are there because they were born there, or married to someone who put them there. Good for them. But also good for you if you're not one of them and are still working your way down the field, yard by yard. These privileged types may get a touchdown first, but their success only requires a short sprint.

Your run takes grit and sweat, and you end up covering a lot more ground

The takeaway from this is that not knowing someone who can help you skip steps can be frustrating. But moving down that field without their help can be exhilarating.

You have every reason to feel good about yourself. Your narrative is as interesting (if not more interesting) as those sunbathing around the pool at the Four Seasons in Maui. My advice is to never get stuck in anger or depression as you witness those riding the nepotism wave. If and/or when you make it on your own, you have every reason to feel superior to them. At least in the moment you cross the goal line. In fact, *gloating* wouldn't be inappropriate. You've just earned the right to be a little smug.

CARRYING THE BURDEN OF AN OX WHILE WALKING ON EGGSHELLS.

*T*HAT'S A LINE FROM Stieg Larsson's *The Girl with the Dragon Tattoo*. It is also a good description of what life as a freelancer can feel like—especially when it comes to finances. Embarking on a career as a freelancer means you're probably, at some stage, going to have cash flow problems. Or worse, be broke and in debt.

Very few freelancers I know have trust funds. For most, especially during those early years of a career, a savings account was considered a luxury item. When you veer off the weekly paycheck routine, there's a good chance the bills will be arriving faster than the cash. The one thing you cannot do in this situation is panic, because panic can tip the scales toward an irreversible loss.

Question is: How do you *not* panic? How do you keep your cool when the IRS is on you for back taxes? When Citi Visa ups your interest rate because you were late on payments? When you drive all the way out to a less than desirable neighborhood to get a small loan from a company whose stock and trade is desperate people— and that doesn't go very well? You flee when faced with their obscenely high interest rates (they didn't mention them on the phone), informing them that legalized theft is still theft. Not that they care. In this economy, there are plenty of people willing to make that deal. It should be noted that you look like a pampered princess in comparison to the other customers looking for loans. Whatever drama these people are dealing with, it seems more likely to involve the term "bail bondsman" than "freelance". You get back in your car and head back to your comfortable neighborhood which you may no longer be able to afford to live in and you wonder how to keep from panicking when you're so far out on the proverbial limb that you can't see the tree trunk.

Before this question is answered, however, another one needs to be poised. This is when you have to stop and be brutally honest with yourself and determine if you're psychologically wired for this kind of instability. If you're one of those people, who—as a kid—dared not color outside the lines, and—as an adult—dare not ever drive over the speed limit, or never dare to throw caution to the wind hoping its aerodynamic, you're probably not a good candidate for a freelance career. But if, after considering all the variables and options, you conclude that you can handle periods of famine because you strongly believe, with good reason, there's a feast out there waiting for you, then you're ready to take steps to quell your anxiety.

The enemy of panic is a to-do list. It doesn't have to be a list of brilliant ideas but it does have to be a list of things that are doable. Since panic leads to a contraction of productivity, by creating a list that is a blueprint for activity you are already weakening panic's hold over you.

The list can be a mix of things to do: calls to make, favors to ask, job leads to follow. At least a few of the items should require a leap of faith. Example: A couple of years ago, when I was spending a lot of time on the furthermost edge of the proverbial limb, I decided to write (on spec) a novel. A decision that could be described as gutsy or delusional considering publishers at the time seemed only interested in buying slick, lifestyle or self-help books from reality television stars, often written by ghost writers—AKA brain doubles. My contemporary spin on historical fiction was not going to inspire a bidding war. Three of my friends had no luck selling their spec novels, and a fourth had but was so disappointed in how it was marketed he and his literary agent parted company and he went back to writing screenplays. I had no literary agent, and finding one was proving to be difficult. Lit agents either want the next new voice with a debut novel or they want a writer with a *New York Times* bestseller track record. What they have no time for is someone whose last book did not sell big numbers. It got to the point where even I had to admit that maybe I wouldn't be able to sell this book right away. Or ever. Still, I continued to search the internet for the names of literary agents who accepted unsolicited manuscripts for consideration. It can be unsettling to send an email and a few chapters of your book (my baby) to someone you not only don't know, but know nothing about except their job title. Not being part of New York's literary world, very few of the names (except the famous ones) meant anything to me. And figuring out who might appreciate my book was really just a roll of the dice. The thing about rolling dice, though, is that eventually if you throw them enough times, your number will inevitably come up. I was lucky enough to find an agent who replied to my initial email within minutes to say she was a big fan of my first novel, *The Cigarette Girl*—and, yes, please send whatever I have. A few months later, she sold the manuscript for *Anne of Hollywood* to Simon & Schuster.

As corny as this to-do list may sound (right now you are starting to feel like you're at some tacky self-help sales conference being held at a second-rate hotel near the airport), it does work. But it requires diligence. When you get to the bottom of the list, write a new one. It's like in basketball when the only way out of a slump is to keep shooting the ball. It's an apt analogy, assuming you have the talent to be on the court in the first place.

There is a caveat that comes with one of the most common entries on the to-do list. Freelancers often turn to a friend if they need a loan or a cosigner for a loan. It's a legitimate approach, but keep this in mind. No one enjoys lending money. It often leads to resentment and broken friendships. If the person you're going to for help is rich, chances are they get hit up for money all the time for all kinds of reasons. I know wealthy men who still get calls for money from women they briefly dated fifteen, twenty years ago. I know successful women who get calls from distant relatives they haven't seen in a decade. Apparently there's no statute of limitation on asking for favors, though perhaps there should be.

Money changing hands is tricky territory, and you have to navigate carefully.

If you're going to ask for a loan, have a plan to pay it back—and stick to it. You can't expect a friend to write you a check just because you're having some financial difficulties and then be okay if it looks like all you're doing is waiting for your luck to turn around. Yes, luck is part of the equation. But when you're using other people's money, you don't have the luxury of waiting around for things to get better. That's when you have to double down on your efforts and be ready to deal with the consequences if you can't pay back the loan in the agreed upon time. The consequences vary, and they include a high risk of losing a friend—and an even higher risk of experiencing waves of self-loathing, which is the last thing any freelancer can afford. Even panic is better than self-loathing.

Another thing on the to-do list is to downsize by moving to a cheaper place. Don't get hung up on how that looks to others. What matters is having the freedom to work on your projects and business, not what others may gossip about. Most successful freelancers have bounced around the map, especially in the early parts of their careers. One year you can afford a house with a view of the Hollywood Hills, the next you're in living in the flats in a one bedroom apartment overlooking a parking lot.

I have an acquaintance, a lawyer, who I run into occasionally, and every time I do he'll say, "Where are you living now?" If I'm not at an upscale address, I can almost hear him thinking, *Poor girl. Things aren't working out for her.* One of these days I might finally say to him,

"Just so you know, down-sizing gives me the time and freedom to work on projects I love rather than living in a posh place and spending too many hours of my week working at a soul-sucking job (as he does) in order to pay for a more prestigious zip code." True, he gets to lounge by his beautiful pool on weekends. But I get to enjoy my work all week long. It's a trade off, and I'm happy with my trade. If I had kids, that would add a different element to this calculation, but I don't. And neither does the lawyer who thinks less of me for not having his hilltop view.

A footnote to that point is this: It's surprising to discover that what you thought you could never live without can be given up fairly easily, without really feeling deprived. Downsizing is a revelation in that department. You might find you don't miss traveling, indulging in exotic vacations, or spending sprees at Barneys. The brain can be re-tooled. Old habits don't have to die painfully. It's amazing how an addiction to freedom and working for yourself can cure you of attachment to anything that jeopardizes that agenda.

Keeping money panic under control might ultimately require coming up with other ways to market your skills. And I'm not talking about screenwriters who make extra cash by working up treatments for other people's ideas, or worse...helping job seekers write-up résumés. My favorite example of branching out is a terrific Hollywood screenwriter known for his ability to write dark, edgy scripts. In the early part of his career he made extra money dabbling in advertising, working with commercial directors to come up with cool ideas for ads. More recently, he's used his knowledge of spiritual psychology (which had always been a passion of his, not a career path) to run well-attended weekly seminars that are a cross between the best college lectures I ever attended and hanging out with friends. Point being: when at all possible—and it's *very* possible—find or create a second niche that gives you access to another source of revenue...without compromising your freelance status.

The takeaway from this is that you got to get good at walking on eggshells. Having to carry a heavy load with a light step is a challenge, not a reason to panic. And if you *do* panic, as a last resort, keep this in mind: Eventually, if you hang in there long enough, even panic gets boring.

RESET

*E*VERY ONE HAS TO hit the reset button from time to time, and freelancers have to hit it more often than most. When you've opted to be your own boss, it means you're the one who has to give yourself the pep talk. You're the designated driver of your own journey. No time to fall asleep at the wheel. It's good to have a plan you can put into action if you find yourself nodding off before the next rest stop.

I can't say my plan is foolproof, but it's helped me climb out of many ruts and helped me a lot more than reading *The Power of Now*. But that's a conversation for another day. My plan has a very silly self-help name: The Three-Point Plan to Reverse a Cosmic Reversal.

You may not have ever heard of a cosmic reversal, but chances are you've experienced one. It's when three bad things happen at the same time. My theory is that when one bad thing happens, it's unfortunate. When two bad things happen at the same time, it's devastating. But when three bad things happen at the same time, life starts to feel Biblical. It's as if you're moving into Book of Job territory and the cosmos has turned against you. Though cosmic reversals don't happen all that often, they happen enough—and in the freelance world, it can go something like this:

You lose a job you were counting on to pay your bills. Your partner on your next project is turning out to be a complete wacko who needs to be medicated. Someone steals your most promising idea and does it in such a way it'll be impossible to prove their guilt and the stress of that gives you an ulcer.

This is when you have to hit the reset button and embrace the three-point plan for recovery.

Step number one is to *snap out of it*. That's a line Cher famously said to Nicolas Cage in the movie *Moonstruck*. In other words, stop wallowing in self-pity and/or negativity. Don't deny negative circumstances, but wallowing is a form of agreeing with the negativity. There's a difference between accepting and agreeing. Nicolas Cage had to accept his past heartbreak, but not agree to a dismal future. Once he snapped out of feeling like a victim, he was liberated from a life stuck in the cellar of that Manhattan bakery and free to enjoy opera in the moonlight with his new love. Snapping out of it—or my preferred version, "snap the fuck out of it"— may not happen overnight. But the second you commit to moving on, the scenery begins to change.

Second step is to count your blessings, and I don't mean that in the usual way—though counting one's blessings in the usual way is a worthwhile endeavor. I mean, take stock of all the things you have going as a way of reconnecting to the foundation of your self-esteem. All the things. That includes people, influences, information, and inspirations. Anything that moves you and has helped you to hone your talent and viewpoint is something to be thankful for because it separates you from the crowd.

Count what you've already accomplished and what you've already overcome. Count those around you who make you laugh, and count those around you who tried but failed to bring you down. Count great sex. Count guilty pleasures. Count something your eighth grade teacher said to you that changed your point of view. Count a piece of music that you connect with in a transformative way. The end game is a highly-tuned sense of your own individuality that will allow you to confidently embrace the motto:

"You can reject me but you can never ever replace me."

That's not arrogance, that's owning your own space in the room.

THE THIRD STEP IS to be courageous about your desires. The first two steps, without this one, will get you headed back in the right direction—but with limited velocity. It is especially when you're trying to reset your emotional alignment that being courageous is so crucial. Every important relationship and career success in my life was the result of moving outside my comfort zone. This is not unusual. Do your own pop quiz. Talk to your friends. Research the bios of successful people. Often courage is key to their story. Often it means thinking differently. Sometimes it means questioning long-held beliefs. Sometimes it means cutting ties. Sometimes it means getting divorced. When you've been crushed by a cosmic reversal, it usually means having the courage to say, "Fuck it. So what? Carry on." It means refusing to be cowered into giving up because things look bleak.

The courageous act doesn't have to be epic. It can be a small step. The goal is to jumpstart your mojo. Example: True story. A young woman—let's call her Elise—who is going through a cosmic reversal (health issue, heartbreak, and financial woes) is invited to a close friend's birthday party. She is expected to give a toast. Speaking in public terrifies her. She has never ever made a toast, and the guest list for this party is approximately eighty people. The thought of getting up and talking in front of eighty people and being required to say something charming and witty seems an impossible task. Since the birthday celebrant is an old friend who has been there for her in moments of need, she doesn't feel she can say no. Even though, in her current state, she feels too shredded to put on a party dress. For weeks leading up to the party, she's a wreck. The anxiety is all-consuming. She rewrites her little speech, practices it, rewrites it again. Finally, the moment comes. Eighty faces focus on her as she stands up to say her piece. Her hand is shaking, and her voice is weak. But she decides to trust her preparation. Not only does she get through the toast, she kills it. The crowd (okay some of them were on their second drink) laughs at her jokes, cheering on her witticisms.

Elise later refers to this toast as "the three-minute speech that changed my life." She was so charged up, having overcome her fear of speaking in public, that she was imbued with confidence—her cosmic reversal temporarily put on hold. So when she saw *him* standing there—a fellow guest, and a man she had always admired but had always been too intimidated to say hello to— she went right up to him and struck up a conversation. Forty-five minutes later, they were still talking. He ended up recommending her for a great job and restoring her fighting spirit. She, jokingly, to this day, refers to him as the *sexy stranger who broke her chain of pain.*

Sometimes hitting the reset button can take you from a cosmic reversal to a cosmic trifecta: Job, Success, Love. Eventually, when you've survived a couple of cosmic reversals, they won't even scare you any more. That's when you become a freelance pro.

WHY BOTHER?

*W*HY BOTHER TRYING TO make it as a freelancer when there are easier ways to survive? It's a question I have been asked by a number of different people over the last twenty years. Most notably, at the start of my career, by one of the smartest business minds in Hollywood. "Why don't you try riding the horse in the direction it's going?" he asked, somewhat incredulous. What he meant was that there are other paths to securing my future that would be far less aggravating than the one I picked.

I assume the paths he was referring to included getting married to a rich guy, getting a normal job—maybe at a studio—and dropping my compulsion to call the shots in my own life. This, from a man who has only called the shots in his own life—so, in effect, he was saying, *You're not me.* And he's right. I will never get to the top of the mountain he climbed, but I can get to the top of the mountain I choose to climb.

Other people have given me similar advice, but unlike Mr. Hollywood Superstar, these people are risk-averse. A freelance life would never appeal to them. Still, their question of "why bother?" is legitimate.

Is the potential upside great enough to make all the suffering worth it?

For twenty years it has been for me—and this is why. There used to be a clear line distinguishing independent contractors from employees, but that line has gotten a lot less defined. It used to be that employees could count on job security if they landed a position at an established company. These days, corporations are shape-shifters. They change as the marketplace requires, and they owe allegiance to no one. These days, it would be wiser to think of yourself as an independent contractor, even if employed at what appears to be a steady job. It makes sense to tailor your career so that there are multiple buyers for your services and your well-being is never put in the hands of one honcho. If you don't do this, you leave yourself vulnerable to the whims of your superiors or to finding yourself on the short end of the deal when there's a shift in corporate policy. The possible exception is working for the government, but if you have the temperament to deal with government bureaucracy you were probably never a good candidate for freelance life in the first place.

I also love the freelance existence because usually there's at least a chance of making big money. In my profession, the big payoff comes if you create a hit television series. That's like owning a little oil well—or a big oil well—if you think about someone like Dick Wolf, who created *Law & Order* and its various spinoffs. As hard as that is to pull off, the fact that it *is* possible is appealing—and exciting. By the way, I don't need a big gushing oil well, but I don't want to feel like that possibility has been taken off the table—which is the case if you end up working for someone else.

Which brings me to the real joy of the freelance life: FREEDOM and inspiration. When you're working for yourself and the goal is to be the best you can be, anything that happens in your life can be applied to improving your business—which is *you*. You are your own science project. It's always easier to strive for your personal best when you're an "independent contractor" and can follow your own vision.

Then there's also the freedom from having to placate those less than inspiring people who have power over you five days a week, every week of the year. Almost everyone I know who has worked at a normal job has a story to tell about some nightmarish department head who is a leverage-abuser with a double digit IQ. Polling my girlfriends, we came up with a Los Angeles stereotype for the nightmares we've endured in the early days of our careers. Picture this: A middle-aged woman, mid-level management type who wears ill-fitting suits, favors spray tans, and has delusions of gradeur because she claims to know one of the women on one of the *Real Housewives* reality shows—or some other manufactured celebrity. She's the type who will deny you your yearly raise for some extremely petty reason, and when you point out that it would have equaled one Starbucks coffee a day and that it isn't really a big loss, she'll make a note in your file about your attitude.

There's also a male stereotype of this kind of leverage-abuser, and he usually drives a car that costs more than he can afford. Beverly Hills is full of guys who live in small, one bedroom apartments, and drive expensive

BMWs. This type expects you to laugh at their unfunny jokes—and if they ever rise to a senior level position, plenty of their underlings will do just that. These guys will give you that raise which equals one Starbucks coffee a day, then practically expect you to kiss their ring for it. It's one thing to be on the receiving end of this when you're twenty-five. To be on the receiving end of it at forty-five is soul-shredding.

That would feel like prison to me. In comparison, as difficult as my freelance career has been, as low as some of my famine moments have been, as terrifying as being perched out on the limb can be, all things considered... *it's been quite a party!*